ys of
the
Christmas Season
2011

Stephanie Collins

Paulist Press
New York/Mahwah, NJ

Cover and book design by Lynn Else

ISBN: 978-0-8091-4717-5

Published by Paulist Press
997 Macarthur Boulevard
Mahwah, New Jersey 07430

www.paulistpress.com

Printed and bound in the
United States of America

November 27
FIRST SUNDAY OF ADVENT

Keep awake!

Advent is a journey. Most journeys are defined by their end-destinations, but in the case of Advent, the end of the journey is Christ himself—an encounter that may come at Christmas, or even before. One person's encounter may occur in the second week of Advent; another's, in the third. Mine may occur today.

We are invited to encounter Christ this season, but if we fail to be attentive at every moment, the actual meeting may pass unnoticed. So we must carve out a place for him, creating in ourselves a Christ-shaped space. In a constant state of watchfulness, we wait for him to appear.

How do I create a Christ-shaped space in myself? What can I do?

Advent discipline: *Each evening this season, on retiring, I will ask myself: When did Christ appear to me today? At what moment? In which person?*

> "Therefore, keep awake—for you do not know when the master of the house will come, in the evening, or at midnight,...or at dawn, or else he may find you asleep when he comes suddenly."
>
> *Mark 13:35–36*

READINGS:
Isa 63:16b–17, 19b; 64:2–7; 1 Cor 1:3–9; Mark 13:33–37

MONDAY, November 28

"Come, let us go up to the mountain of the LORD,
  to the house of the God of Jacob;
that he may teach us his ways
  and that we may walk in his paths."

Isaiah 2:3

In the Bible, mountaintops are places where one comes close to God and where life-changing events occur. Recall Mount Sinai where Moses received the tablets of the Law, or Mount Nebo from whose top Moses beheld the promised land, or the mount of the transfiguration, or Golgotha.

We approach the mountain of our own transformation with a sense of purpose. We have a need to go up because we long to put ourselves in God's hands. What God may ask or reveal to us at the top may surprise us, but it will definitely shape our future.

What would I *seek in a mountaintop encounter with God? What am I looking for? Let me name it.*

The healing of the centurion's servant in today's gospel took place after Jesus "had come down from the mountain" (Matt 8:1). It is an example of the way Jesus turned his mountaintop experience into action.

READINGS:
Isa 2:1–5; Matt 8:5–11

TUESDAY, November 29

With the eyes of a child

We live in a world of "spin," where all things are interpreted and nothing is clear. Newspapers, news sites, talk shows, and politicians set people against each other, disparage motives, and create smoke screens in order to obscure the real situation. In such a climate, those who are defenseless and the least articulate become the losers.

The Messiah, when he comes, will not judge by putting his spin on things.

> He shall not judge by what his eyes see,
> or decide by what his ears hear;
> but with righteousness he shall judge the poor,
> and decide with equity for the meek of the
> earth.
>
> *Isaiah 11:3–4*

Sometimes we ask ourselves, "What would Jesus do?" Today let me ask, "How would Jesus judge?" In one, concrete social situation, let me try to see without guile—as though with the eyes of a child—and to give voice to what is really happening.

> "Blessed are the eyes that see what you see!"
>
> *Luke 10:23*

READINGS:
Isa 11:1–10; Luke 10:21–24

WEDNESDAY, November 30
ANDREW, APOSTLE

Becoming an apostle

Today's readings make a connection between believing and proclaiming the truth. Peter and Andrew in today's gospel are summoned to believe in Christ and to follow him—to become his apostles. Like them, we are summoned to acknowledge Christ in the world, thereby inspiring others. In this way, the process of being called, following, and proclaiming is replicated over and over.

This doesn't mean we must suddenly become public preachers. However, a faith that doesn't flower into some kind of public acknowledgment is no faith at all. Like it or not, being a Christian involves giving testimony—at least implicitly—to the truth we hold. One can't follow Christ without becoming his apostle.

When did I last take a position that was anchored on my faith in God? Let me recall that moment and celebrate it.

> How beautiful are the feet of those who bring good news.
>
> *Romans 10:15*

READINGS:
Rom 10:9–18; Matt 4:18–22

THURSDAY, December 1

Open the gates,
so that the righteous nation that keeps the faith
may enter in.

Isaiah 26:2

We each in our own way build a wall around the city of our heart. The wall is reassuring, because we desire to control what comes into our city—to admit the good and exclude the evil. But Jesus tells us, beware! Constantly reexamine your choices, since the thing you exclude could be the very thing that brings you life.

Walls that are built of anger and ignorance must be pulled down. If not, says Jesus, the rain and wind will undermine them, and they will collapse. In the end, openness is the ideal.

For he has brought low
the inhabitants of that height;
the lofty city he lays low.

Isaiah 26:5

Who or what am I excluding that might give me life?

The foot tramples it,
the feet of the poor,
the steps of the needy.

Isaiah 26:6

READINGS:
Isa 26:1–6; Matt 7:21, 24–27

FRIDAY, December 2
WORLD AIDS DAY

Reversals of fortune

Isaiah promises there will be reversals of fortune when the messiah comes: the tyrant will be overthrown, the scoffer will come to believe, the blind will see, and the deaf hear.

> Shall not Lebanon in a very little while
> become a fruitful field,
> and the fruitful field be regarded as a forest?
>
> *Isaiah 29:17*

The real challenge is to see the potential for growth in people we encounter. One tries to discern the hunger for faith in the heart of the skeptic, the capacity for doing good in the down-and-out street person, the potential for greatness in the baby born to immigrant parents. We wish to see these people as God sees them. If we remain blind to the possibilities in people, most likely we will resist the reversal of fortune the messiah will bring to fruition.

Today I will ask God to open my eyes to the hidden potential of one particular person in my life.

> "According to your faith, let it be done to you."
> And their eyes were opened.
>
> *Matthew 9:29–30*

READINGS:
Isa 29:17–24; Matt 9:27–31

SATURDAY, December 3
FRANCIS XAVIER, PRIEST

The Lord of Compassion

Matthew tells us that when Jesus saw the crowds that swarmed around him, "he had compassion for them because they were...like sheep without a shepherd" (Matt 9:36). How do sheep behave when they have no shepherd? Disorganized? Frightened? Lost? In any event, it was enough to stir the heart of Jesus. His presence comforted and protected them.

We all have days when we are like those sheep. There are days when we forget to look to Jesus as our shepherd and we assume that everything depends on us alone. Gradually we become frightened, lost, unsure of ourselves. However, the compassion of Jesus is never-ending. In our darkest hours, he reaches out still and says, "Rest in me. Be safe with me."

What is most worrisome in my life right now? Let me place it in the hands of Jesus, my shepherd.

> Though the Lord may give you the bread of
> adversity and the water of affliction, yet your
> Teacher will not hide himself any more, but your
> eyes shall see your Teacher.
>
> *Isaiah 30:20*

READINGS:
Isa 30:19–21, 23–26; Matt 9:35—10:1, 5a, 6–8

December 4
Second Sunday of Advent

Advent embraces the coming of Jesus in history two thousand years ago, while simultaneously embracing the coming of Jesus at the end of time, when there will be "new heavens and a new earth, where righteousness is at home" (2 Pet 3:13). These two realities are joined in the life of the individual Christian who *believes* in the Jesus of history and *models* the Jesus who is to come.

When we give God's righteousness a home in ourselves, Jesus will at last appear for all to see. In this way we each become another John the Baptizer, creating space for Jesus to appear. Like John, we must recognize him, point him out, name him.

Today, take five minutes while walking or driving, look around, and then consciously put Jesus in the world that is waiting for him.

> "I am sending my messenger ahead of you,
> who will prepare your way;
> the voice of one crying out in the wilderness;
> 'Prepare the way of the Lord,
> make his paths straight.'"
>
> *Mark 1:2*

Readings:
Isa 40:1–5, 9–11; 2 Pet 3:8–14; Mark 1:1–8

MONDAY, December 5

The desert shall blossom!

A powerful current of joy surges through this day's readings. They assure us that our dry places will come to life again; our paralyses of inaction will be healed; our sins will be forgiven.

> The wilderness and the dry land shall be glad,
> the desert shall rejoice and blossom;
> like the crocus it shall blossom abundantly.
>
> *Isaiah 35:1–2*

The only action we need to take is to lay our hurts before God—in the same way that the paralyzed man was lowered through a hole in the roof in today's gospel and laid before Jesus. Jesus is waiting to flood our arid souls with the water of grace. This water will reach our deepest places to make us spiritually supple and fresh.

What dry, paralyzed places do I have that are waiting for God's healing?

> Then the lame shall leap like a deer,
> and the tongue of the speechless sing for joy.
>
> *Isaiah 35:5*

READINGS:
Isa 35:1–10; Luke 5:17–26

TUESDAY, December 6
Nicholas, Bishop

Nicholas was a fourth-century bishop in Myra, a city in modern-day Turkey, who, it was said, secretly gave gifts of money to the poor. His example so inspired followers that after his death they continued his practice of gift giving. For us, Nicholas is an exemplar of Christian compassion that consciously seeks out the needy and helps them.

Poor and lost people have a special claim on us. Jesus said, "Truly I tell you, [the shepherd] rejoices over [the lost sheep that has been found] more than over the ninety-nine that never went astray" (Matt 18:13).

> He will feed his flock like a shepherd;
>   he will gather the lambs in his arms,
> and carry them in his bosom,
>   and gently lead the mother sheep.
>
> *Isaiah 40:11*

Readings:
Isa 40:1–11; Matt 18:12–14

WEDNESDAY, December 7
AMBROSE, BISHOP AND DOCTOR OF THE CHURCH

Weariness!

Weariness stalks us this time of the year. The days are getting short and our tasks are many. The weeks leading up to Christmas, which ought to be a time of quiet, joyful preparation, are anything but quiet. Our calendar is crammed with social plans and events, with shopping and card writing—in addition to the regular stuff going on.

It is faint comfort to be told in today's readings that although we grow weary, God does not. "He does not faint or grow weary; his understanding is unsearchable" (Isa 40:28). Easy for him to say.

God is blessed with the long view. Our view of things is short, conditional, and often confused. God invites us today to see things his way, from the perspective of eternity. When we do, our tasks don't disappear, but they become suddenly less weighty.

Stop and reflect: What is God's view of my schedule and plans for today?

> "Come to me, all you that are weary and are carrying heavy burdens, and I will give you rest. Take my yoke upon you, and learn from me...and you will find rest for your souls."
>
> *Matthew 11:28–29*

READINGS:
Isa 40:25–31; Matt 11:28–30

THURSDAY, December 8
THE IMMACULATE CONCEPTION

Becoming a vessel

Coming as it does in the early days of Advent, this feast of Mary directs us to reflect on her role in the history of salvation. People often misinterpret the mystery of this feast, and today's gospel inadvertently confirms that misunderstanding. It is not the conception of Jesus that we celebrate but Mary's own conception—her emergence as a vessel suitable for birthing God.

Along with John the Baptizer, Mary is a model for what we need to become. Each of us in our own way and in our own good time can be a vessel. We prepare the soil of our person. We try to live as much as possible with pure hearts. This work is pleasing in God's eyes. In time, we may find life growing within us, a life that is not us but greater than us—something altogether New.

It is the process of preparation that we honor today—that "Mary" part of us—the slow, laborious, but fruitful process of becoming a vessel.

Today I will picture myself as a vessel, empty and waiting.

> "Here am I, the servant of the Lord; let it be with me according to your word."
>
> *Luke 1:38*

READINGS:
Gen 3:9–15, 20; Eph 1:3–6, 11–12; Luke 1:26–38

FRIDAY, December 9
JUAN DIEGO, HERMIT

According to legend, when Juan Diego climbed to the top of a hill, as directed by Mary in an apparition, he found roses growing there. Roses in midwinter! He gathered them in his cloak and carried them to his bishop.

Roses in winter can be a metaphor for grace during cold, bleak times. For us to find grace amid hardship, we have to be looking for it, waiting for it. Since he was a hermit—a man attentive to God—Juan Diego was alert to the treasure when it appeared. Alertness is the key.

Am I as attentive as I should be to God's voice? Today, in a quiet moment, I will ask God, "What do you wish to give me?"

> O that you had paid attention to my
> commandments!
> Then your prosperity would have been like a
> river,
> and your success like the waves of the sea.
>
> *Isaiah 48:18*

READINGS:
Isa 48:17–19; Matt 11:16–19

SATURDAY, December 10

The appointed time

The great Western faiths are all "historical religions": they believe that God is revealed in history at particular times and places. The Epistle to the Galatians declares that Jesus appeared "in the fullness of time" (Gal 4:4). Today in the Book of Sirach we read that the messiah will appear "at the appointed time." Both of these texts suggest that a state of readiness at a particular moment is a precondition if God is to appear.

In point of fact, God comes over and over. On most occasions we fail to recognize him because our time is so cluttered and disconnected. It is up to us to create a moment of "fullness" for God. If I want Jesus to be born into me this Christmas of 2011, then I must prepare a place for him. I must clean the stable of my heart, lay fresh straw in the manger, open the doors, and wait.

What is interfering with my perception this year? Let me set those things aside for a moment today and create a space for God.

> At the appointed time, it is written, you are destined
> to calm the wrath of God...
> and to restore the tribes of Jacob.
>
> *Sirach 48:10*

READINGS:
Sir 48:1–4, 9–11; Matt 17:9a, 10–13

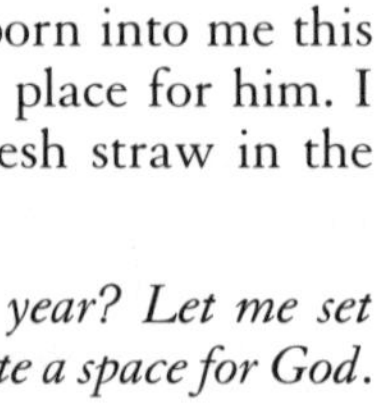

December 11
THIRD SUNDAY OF ADVENT

Rejoice always, pray without ceasing.
1 Thessalonians 5:16

In this third week of Advent, the mood of expectation ratchets up. Today the readings tell us to rejoice, then in the same breath urge us to keep praying. It's enough to make one dizzy with multitasking.

But along with the multiple commands flows a strong undercurrent of joy. The Messiah is already among us, but unseen. "Among you stands one whom you do not know," the gospel announces (John 1:26). And again: "The true light, which enlightens everyone, was coming into the world" (John 1:9).

We need to keep our heads amid all this giddiness of expectation. Take a deep breath. Remain happy, but wait. We must let Christmas grow in us and come to full flower—a process that can't be rushed.

Today I will try to do simple things—ordinary things—like cleaning my room or writing notes to friends, conscious all the while that Christ is growing within.

For as the earth brings forth its shoots…
so the Lord GOD will cause righteousness and
praise
to spring up before all the nations.
Isaiah 61:11

READINGS:
Isa 61:1–2a, 10–11; 1 Thess 5:16–24; John 1:6–8, 19–28

MONDAY, December 12
OUR LADY OF GUADALUPE

The God of surprises

Both of today's readings—from Luke and from the prophet Zechariah—recount visits from angels. In both cases the person being visited is puzzled and filled with questions about the nature of the visit. Luke tells us that Mary was "perplexed" by the angel Gabriel's words. She asked, "How can this be?" (Luke 1:29, 34). In a similar manner, Zechariah kept questioning his own angelic visitor.

God's ways are not ours. We expect God to work in one way and are surprised when he chooses a different approach. It adds to his mystery and is part of his charm. It also serves to remind us that we don't know what is best either for our world or for ourselves. Those who await God at Advent or at any other time must be humble and expect the unexpected.

Am I stalled in some life situation because I have a predetermined notion of how it ought to turn out? How can I let go of my expectations?

> Sing and rejoice, O daughter Zion! See, I am
> coming to dwell among you.
>
> *Zechariah 2:14 (NAB)*

READINGS:
Zech 2:14–17; Luke 1:26–38

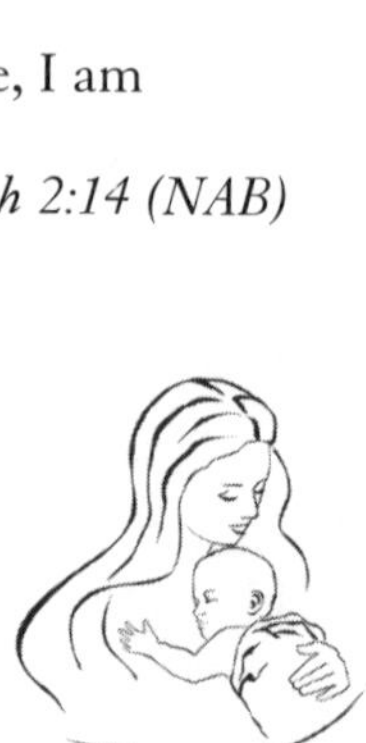

TUESDAY, December 13
LUCY, VIRGIN AND MARTYR

Ah, soiled, defiled, oppressing city!

Zephaniah 3:1

One of the hardest things about being a professed Christian is dealing with the dysfunction—even sinfulness—of the church. There is often a chasm between the ideals that church people and its leaders profess to stand for and what they actually do. It is no different now than in the time of Jesus, who warned religious leaders of his day that "tax collectors and the prostitutes are going into the kingdom of God ahead of you" (Matt 21:31).

We have a responsibility as believers to help our church conform to the gospel. It is neither a progressive task nor a conservative one: it is a Christian task. We can do it first by personal example. We must be, ourselves, what we want our church to be. But the responsibility can also embrace reform movements and public acts of solidarity. If we liken the church to the stable, shouldn't we work to make it more suitable for the Lord and those who come to worship him?

What concrete thing can I do this Advent to make my church a place where God shines out to the world?

I will leave in the midst of you
a people humble and lowly.
They shall seek refuge in the name of the
LORD—
the remnant of Israel.

Zephaniah 3:12–13

READINGS:
Zeph 3:1–2, 9–13; Matt 21:28–32

WEDNESDAY, December 14
JOHN OF THE CROSS, DOCTOR OF THE CHURCH

"Go and tell John what you have seen and heard."
Luke 7:22

When John's followers asked Jesus if he was "the one who is to come" (Luke 7:20), Jesus answered by recounting the good works he had done in God's name: healing the sick, preaching the good news, and so on. In this way we understand how loving service to the needy reveals God's presence. It is true today as well. The best answers one can give to unbelievers in our own day are acts of love.

And yet, when confronted by skeptics, how often do we try to win over the other side by arguing with them or quoting scripture rather than letting our own loving service be the answer? Putting it that way, how well have our recent lives modeled the compassion of Jesus?

Reflect: If people looked to me as a model of loving Christian service, what might they conclude?

Let the skies rain down righteousness;
let the earth open, that salvation may spring up.
Isaiah 45:8

READINGS:
Isa 45:6b–8, 18, 21b–25; Luke 7:18b–23

THURSDAY, December 15

Steadfast love

Advent is a time when we pretend we are waiting for God, but all the while God is really waiting for us. During those moments when he seems to be far away, when we feel empty and uncertain, God is actually close by, waiting for us to awaken. We are never alone. As Isaiah writes:

> For the mountains may depart
>   and the hills be removed,
> but my steadfast love shall not depart from you,
>   and my covenant of peace shall not be removed,
>   says the Lord.
>
> *Isaiah 54:10*

Because our own love is so imperfect, lukewarm, and fickle, we project those qualities onto God. Not so. It is a challenge for us to swallow our pride and accept a love that is lavished on us regardless of our faults.

Today, I will take a moment simply to sit and let God's love wash over me, then find an appropriate word of thanks.

> With everlasting love I will have compassion on you,
>   says the Lord, your Redeemer.
>
> *Isaiah 54:8*

READINGS:
Isa 54:1–10; Luke 7:24–30

FRIDAY, December 16

Doing the faith

Christians too often look upon "the faith" as a collection of tenets we ascribe to. We talk about "the content of faith" as if it were kept in a strongbox somewhere. Jesus, on the other hand, tends to speak of faith as a kind of activity rooted in commitment. To people who questioned him about his mission, he said, "The very works that I am doing testify on my behalf that the Father has sent me" (John 5:36).

Thus, it would seem that "holding" the faith is less important than "doing" it. Indeed, if we accept everything in the *Catechism* but fail to follow it, our faith is empty.

Great deeds are not required. Today in the Book of Isaiah, God declares that the simplest and most humble actions are sufficient:

> All who keep the sabbath, and do not profane it,
> and hold fast to my covenant—
> these I will bring to my holy mountain,
> and make them joyful in my house of prayer.
>
> *Isaiah 56:6–7*

How great is the disconnect between what I believe and how I behave? Today I will try to let my actions speak as my faith.

READINGS:
Isa 56:1–3a, 6–8; John 5:33–36

SATURDAY, December 17

> Jesus the Messiah, the son of David, the son of Abraham...
>
> *Matthew 1:1*

The genealogy of Jesus as recounted by Matthew in today's gospel records the step-by-step progress of salvation through the ages—through periods when it seemed as though God's plan had been thwarted and was going nowhere—until at last on a darkened hillside in Bethlehem, it blossomed in the person of Jesus Christ.

From this we learn that history is purposeful—God's history and our own. Most likely there were stretches in our lives when it seemed our original purpose was lost and our efforts pointless. Yet all this time God was preparing us, step-by-step, for glory.

God's story is our story. Our personal history is purposeful. Today, even as we prepare for the arrival of the Savior, God is readying a manger for our birth.

Today, with my end-purpose in mind, I will pray: "O Wisdom, O holy Word of God, come and show your people the way to salvation."

READINGS:
Gen 49:2, 8–10; Matt 1:1–17

December 18
Fourth Sunday of Advent

"Greetings, favored one!"

This evening in the O Antiphons, we appeal to the "sacred Lord of ancient Israel," thereby identifying Jesus with the awaited Messiah and uniting our Advent with the expectations of the Jewish people down through the ages. By this fourth week, one is beginning to feel the wait for God is very long, even tedious. Imagine how it seemed to the Jews.

God will be there to greet us at the end, but we must remember that God is also *in* the waiting. As we hear today in the Second Book of Samuel, "I have been with you wherever you went" (2 Sam 7:9). One can't reach the destination without doing the journey. Indeed, in the lifetime of waiting, we slowly become "favored ones," capable of receiving the Messiah.

We are comforted by the assurance that our long labor will plant God's kingdom more firmly in history, where succeeding generations can see it flower.

Today, I will thank God for the privilege of living in expectation.

> I will raise up your offspring after you, who shall come forth from your body,...and I will establish the throne of his kingdom forever.
>
> *2 Samuel 7:12–13*

Readings:
2 Sam 7:1–5, 8b–12, 14a, 16; Rom 16:25–27; Luke 1:26–38

MONDAY, December 19

Let us reflect on new life that comes to dead places

The antiphon at evening prayer hails the "flower from Jesse's stem." In fact, Isaiah uses the phrase "Jesse's stump" to describe how new growth can sprout from a ruined tree (11:1). We recall that Jesse was the father of David, and that David—the ancestor of Jesus—grew to become the king of Israel.

Developing this theme, today's readings describe how Elizabeth in her old age conceived a child, who became John the Baptist. A parallel story from the Book of Judges relates how another woman—nameless, referred to only as the wife of Manoah—likewise conceived a son, who became the warrior and tribal leader Samson. Both women had been elderly and barren, yet both brought forth new life.

In which of my dead places is God preparing to bring forth new life? Will it be in me personally, or in my church, or in society—or in all of these? Let me ponder the question and wait for the angel who will reveal the answer to me.

> O Flower of Jesse's stem,...come, let nothing keep you from coming to our aid.
>
> *Antiphon, Evening Prayer*

READINGS:
Judg 13:2–7, 24–25a; Luke 1:5–25

TUESDAY, December 20

The Lord will give a sign

In today's gospel, we remember Mary's being called by the angel Gabriel. Mary is often revered as a model of the church as a whole. Like the church, she was chosen to bear the Savior and present him to the world. The Litany of Loreto gives her the title "Ark of the Covenant." She bore Christ, as the Jewish ark bore the covenant of Israel.

By nice coincidence, today at sunset marks the beginning of Hanukkah, when Jews around the world celebrate the rededication of the Temple in Jerusalem, which happened two centuries before Christ. According to pious legend, there was only enough oil to keep the sanctuary light at the new Temple burning for twenty-four hours, but somehow it burned for six days. It was a sign.

God gives us signs for a purpose. Mary's selection was a sign. Perhaps each one of us —if we let God work through us—is intended to be a sign to the world.

How might I be a sign to the world? What must I do so that my very being reveals that "God is with us"?

> "The Lord himself will give you a sign. Look, the
> young woman is with child and shall bear a son,
> and shall name him Immanuel."
>
> *Isaiah 7:14*

READINGS:
Isa 7:10–14; Luke 1:26–38

WEDNESDAY, December 21
PETER CANISIUS, BISHOP AND DOCTOR OF THE CHURCH

For now the winter is past,
the rain is over and gone.
The flowers appear on the earth;
the time of singing has come.

Song of Songs 2:11–12

As we approach the shortest, darkest day of the year, it sounds odd to have readings describing verdant springtime when the fallow earth pours forth a rich abundance of life. Of course we know that even when the ground is frozen, our roots maintain the spark of life and will one day stir. Cold and darkness will not prevail. On this day, especially, we hold fast to the belief that God has the desire and the means to make it happen.

Where in my life has the cold become entrenched and growth stalled? Today in prayer I will bring that place to God and ask the Divine Gardener to send light and nourishment so that my barren place may flower.

"Blessed are you among women, and blessed is the fruit of your womb."

Luke 1:42

READINGS:
Song 2:8–14; Luke 1:39–45

THURSDAY, December 22

The Mighty One does great things

God's ways are not ours. Desiring to free the human race from the wallow of sin and hopelessness, God did not entrust the task to "experts" or seek out "the best minds" to get it done. As a way of showing that this was really God's doing, the work of salvation was handed over to a pregnant teenager, a small-town carpenter, a ragtag collection of fishermen, a few shepherds, a tax collector, and, last of all, you and me.

Each of us in our own way can appreciate Mary's song of gratitude: "The Mighty One has done great things for me, and holy is his name" (Luke 1:49). Having been lifted up, though, let us beware of getting inflated egos or imagining that we, all by ourselves, are powerful and wise. To be fruitful, our work relies on God's sustaining hand.

Which task confronting me today is being done for personal glory? How can I turn it into God's work?

> O King of all the nations,...O Keystone of the mighty arch of humanity, come and save the creature you fashioned from the dust.
>
> *Antiphon, Evening Prayer*

READINGS:
1 Sam 1:24–28; Luke 1:46–56

FRIDAY, December 23
JOHN OF KANTY, PRIEST

The sense that God is preparing us for a test or trial pervades today's readings. First, the prophet Malachi warns that "the Lord...will suddenly come into his temple" (Mal 3:1), and it won't be an easy time for anyone. For the faithful, the Lord's arrival will demand personal purification in much the same way that silver is melted down and refined by fire.

Next, Luke recounts how Zechariah, the husband of Elizabeth, went through such a trial. He was deprived of the power of speech during her pregnancy. Not until he and Elizabeth brought the child to be circumcised was Zechariah's mouth opened and his tongue freed, "and he began to speak, praising God" (Luke 1:64).

In our day, Christmas has been sanitized: a holiday of jolly Santas and prancing reindeer. One would believe there are no tests left to endure. Be warned, however. The coming of the Lord will confront each of us with a choice: Yes or No?

Will my answer be yes? And what will that mean for the way I live my life?

> O Emmanuel, desire of the nations, come and set
> us free, Lord our God.
>
> *Antiphon, Evening Prayer*

READINGS:
Mal 3:1–4, 23–24; Luke 1:57–66

SATURDAY, December 24

Dawn will break

Sometimes the only thing we can do during a hard time is wait it out. We latch onto the slender hope that eventually hard times will end. Then, after waiting and hoping through the long hours of night, we see the first streaks of dawn appear in the eastern sky. Ah, what a premonition of joy touches us then! It is a fragile joy—not yet fully realized—but still a joy!

As surely as the sun rises in the east, we can be sure that God will come to our aid. God, to quote St. Augustine, has "made us for himself." God would not have given us a body, or desires, or a history if he had not fully intended to make a home with us.

Let me ready myself for joy. The Visitor is walking toward my door, reaching up his hand to knock, while I stand just inside. Let me be fully alive to this moment.

> "The dawn from on high will break upon us,
> to give light to those who sit in darkness and in the
> shadow of death,
> to guide our feet into the way of peace."
>
> *Luke 1:78–79*

MORNING READINGS:
2 Sam 7:1–5, 8b–12, 14a, 16; Luke 1:67–79

SUNDAY, December 25
THE NATIVITY OF THE LORD

Long ago God spoke to our ancestors in many and various ways by the prophets, but in these last days he has spoken to us by a Son.

Hebrews 1:1

Alleluia!

Christian, remember your dignity, and now that you share in God's own nature, do not return by sin to your former base condition. Bear in mind who is your head and of whose body you are a member. Do not forget that you have been rescued from the power of darkness and brought into the light of God's kingdom.

Pope Leo the Great, from
the Christmas Office of Readings

Alleluia!

And the Word was made flesh and lived among us,
and we have seen his glory, the glory as of a father's
only son,
full of grace and truth.

John 1:14

Alleluia!

READINGS:
Isa 52:7–10; Heb 1:1–6; John 1:1–18

MONDAY, December 26
STEPHEN, THE FIRST MARTYR

Giving him away

Jesus came on earth to be given away. We are not supposed to possess him: to lock him away in our hearts as a personal and private savior. We are supposed to let him loose: to give him to the world as Mary did with the infant Jesus at Bethlehem.

Stephen, a deacon in the church of Jerusalem, knew this to be true. By his preaching, he made Jesus come alive among his listeners. According to the Acts of the Apostles, "Stephen, full of grace and power," opened himself up and proclaimed the Word of God in a world that waited fearfully to hear it (Acts 6:8).

Do I sometimes treat Jesus as a possession that is meant for me alone? Do I hold onto him too tightly? How can I liberate him so that others may encounter him and come to believe?

> Yesterday our king, clothed in his robe of flesh, left his place in the virgin's womb and graciously visited the world. Today his soldier [Stephen] leaves the tabernacle of his body and goes triumphantly to heaven.
>
> *Office of Readings*

READINGS:
Acts 6:8–10; 7:54–59; Matt 10:17–22

TUESDAY, December 27
JOHN, APOSTLE AND EVANGELIST

> We declare to you what was from the beginning, what we have heard, what we have seen with our eyes, what we have looked at and touched with our hands, concerning the word of life.
>
> *1 John 1:1*

Picture this: On Easter morning, the apostles sprint to the tomb to verify Mary Magdalen's story of having encountered the risen Jesus. John, being young and swift, arrives first and sees that the stone has been rolled away. He steps aside to let Peter enter, then he follows. They are astonished. The body of Jesus is gone.

Such moments of firsthand knowledge happen infrequently in our lives. We need to seize on them and remember them. When people ask us what we believe and why, let us no longer just spout Christian doctrine or enumerate the teachings of the church. We, too, are called to be witnesses of the risen Christ.

Let me remember a moment of astonishment in my life, and quietly give thanks for it.

> We declare to you what we have seen and heard so that you also may have fellowship with us.
>
> *1 John 1:3*

READINGS:
1 John 1:1–4; John 20:1a, 2–8

WEDNESDAY, December 28
THE HOLY INNOCENTS, MARTYRS

If we say we have no sin…

Don't blame the massacre on Herod alone. Our age is also guilty of violence against innocent children. Think, for a minute, of children caught in the crossfire of war and terrorism. Think of those innocents who have been aborted, or—perhaps even worse—the "soul-murder" of children who have suffered sexual abuse. The slaughter of the innocents continues in our age unabated, perhaps even at a quickened pace. "If we say that we have no sin, we deceive ourselves, and the truth is not in us" (1 John 1:8).

So let us not be deceived. Or rather, let us un-deceive ourselves and admit what is going on in our age. Our personal salvation may depend upon our acknowledging the truth and throwing ourselves on God's mercy.

What acts of violence against the innocent have I been ignoring? How, concretely, can I help these innocent ones?

> If we confess our sins, he who is faithful and just will forgive us our sins and cleanse us from all unrighteousness.
>
> *1 John 1:9*

READINGS:
1 John 1:5—2:2; Matt 2:13–18

THURSDAY, December 29
THOMAS BECKET, BISHOP AND MARTYR

The days immediately after Christmas, which ought to be so joyful, are suddenly fraught with blood and sacrifice. First we encountered Stephen, then the Holy Innocents, and now Thomas Becket, who was brutally murdered in Canterbury Cathedral for opposing his king. The three feasts taken together seem to be warning us that the reign of God is not going to be easy. We don't need a calendar to know that these are the darkest days of the year.

That death and darkness—and fear and anger—stalk the earth should not come as a surprise. We cower before it, yet the coming of Christ has given us another option: to spurn it and cling to the light in the midst of darkness. As today's readings tell us "Whoever hates another…is in the darkness, walks in the darkness,…because the darkness has brought on blindness" (1 John 2:11).

Events in the world provide ample reasons to be fearful and angry. Do I find myself slipping under their spell? How can I let go of anger and fear and be attentive to Christ?

> "My eyes have seen your salvation,
> which you have prepared in the presence of all peoples."
>
> *Luke 2:30–31*

READINGS:
1 John 2:3–11; Luke 2:22–35

FRIDAY, December 30
THE HOLY FAMILY OF JESUS, MARY, AND JOSEPH

Bear with one another

It's not easy to live in community. The business of getting along with others and fitting our lives into theirs is challenging and humbling. Whether the community is our birth family, our family of marriage, or our religious community, the dynamics are essentially the same. The family grates on us; our rough edges are slowly smoothed away. We emerge from the experience diminished—and yet somehow *enlarged*.

Today's readings contain much practical advice about getting along in family settings. According to Sirach:

> Accept whatever befalls you,
> and in times of humiliation be patient.
> For gold is tested in the fire...
> in the furnace of humiliation.
>
> *Sirach 2:5*

What do I find irksome about family life? Could my annoyance with my family be a form of resistance to God's invitation? Let me reflect prayerfully on this.

> Bear with one another and, if anyone has a complaint against another, forgive each other; just as the Lord has forgiven you, so you also must forgive.
>
> *Colossians 3:13*

READINGS:
Sir 3:2–7, 12–14; Col 3:12–21; Luke 2:22–40

SATURDAY, December 31
SYLVESTER I, POPE

> From his fullness we have all received, grace upon grace.
>
> *John 1:16*

Today's readings celebrate the way God holds us in a divine embrace, lavishing gifts and blessings on us. We are showered with graces, anointed by the Spirit, and taken into God's family where we are cherished as children—not as infants, but as adult sons and daughters.

To be numbered among God's chosen ones is a great gift. No one can take that privilege from us: no earthly force, not even death. At the end of this eventful year, we can rest in that certainty.

Today let my prayer be, "I am yours, Lord God, and you are mine. We belong to each other."

> You have been anointed by the Holy One, and all of you have knowledge.
>
> *1 John 2:20*

READINGS:
1 John 2:18–21; John 1:1–18

SUNDAY, January 1
MARY, MOTHER OF GOD

God's name, my name

The act of giving and accepting a name is deeply meaningful in all world religions. By bestowing a name, we recognize the other's identity and enter into relationship—discovering in the process our own identity as well.

We are told that the angel at Bethlehem called the newborn child "Savior" and "Messiah," descriptions that Mary "pondered...in her heart" (Luke 2:19). The First Council of Ephesus in the year 491 declared that Mary—and, through her, the whole human race—was *Theotokos*, or "God-bearer." This intimate connection bestows on each of us the right to call God "Abba."

Reflect prayerfully: What name do I bestow on the transcendent God? What name does God bestow on me? Let me spend time just resting in these words we speak to one another.

> God has sent the Spirit of his Son into our hearts, crying "Abba! Father!" So you are no longer a slave but a child, and if a child then also an heir.
>
> *Galatians 4:6–7*

READINGS:
Num 6:22–27; Gal 4:4–7; Luke 2:16–21

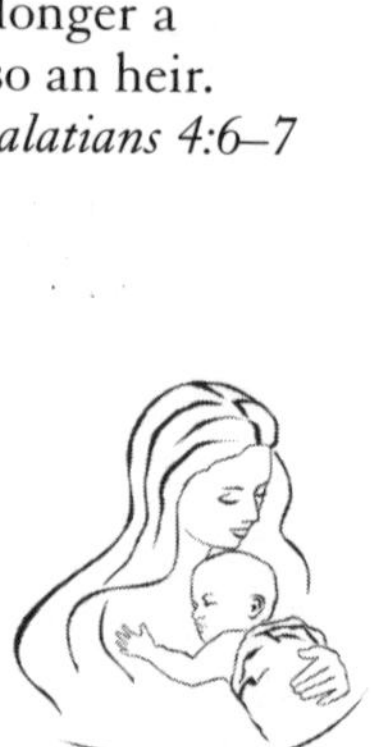

MONDAY, January 2
Basil the Great and Gregory Nazianzen, Bishops and Doctors of the Church

When the priests and Levites asked John why he baptized those who came to him by the Jordan, he explained, "I baptize with water" (John 1:26). Without quite saying so, he implied that his was a simple kind of baptism, using ordinary water. It was not the baptism of the Spirit, nor was it immersion into Jesus' death and resurrection—obviously, because at that point Jesus had not yet been put to death.

Our lives are comprised of many ordinary actions that seem to have no religious significance. Ours is a state of everyday grace. It is enough for us to baptize with water. In time, we hope, Jesus will invest our simple gestures with transformative meaning so that we will be able to look back on all that we've done and see our lives aglow with divinity.

On this first day of the year, let me reflect and be content with the everyday quality of my life. It is not for me to claim anything special for myself. Let me surrender entirely to God.

"Among you stands one whom you do not know."
John 1:26

Readings:
1 John 2:22–28; John 1:19–28

TUESDAY, January 3
THE MOST HOLY NAME OF JESUS

Any moment now

Any moment now, we may encounter salvation. It may seem like an ordinary moment—an ordinary encounter—but in that moment, grace can be loosed on the world. That's the way it was for John, baptizing along the Jordan. A myriad of faces—people waiting to be baptized—then, suddenly, one of them was Jesus.

> "I myself did not know him; but I came baptizing with water for this reason, that he might be revealed."
>
> *John 1:31*

Our task is to be attentive to the presence of grace and give it a name when it appears. We do this for our friends and neighbors, and we do it for ourselves—we name the grace. We reveal God standing in our midst for those who cannot see.

Today God's face may shine forth from an ordinary encounter. Let me be ready to name it when it happens.

> What we do know is this: when he is revealed, we will be like him, for we will see him as he is.
>
> *1 John 3:2*

READINGS:
1 John 2:29—3:6; John 1:29–34

WEDNESDAY, January 4
ELIZABETH ANN SETON, RELIGIOUS

In these days leading up to Epiphany, the daily readings concentrate on ways we encounter Jesus. With John, it happened suddenly while he was baptizing along the Jordan. In other accounts, Jesus sought out disciples, as he will Philip in tomorrow's readings. In today's example, the initiative rests with the disciples themselves. Andrew and a friend see Jesus passing by and decide to follow him.

In all of these cases, seekers have an inarticulate need that only Jesus is able to fulfill. These are people who are not content with ordinary existence. They want Something More. This doesn't mean ordinary life is bad, but it does suggest that serious seekers look beyond the usual comforts of life and keep their eyes on the ultimate good. Each day they recommit themselves to the search.

What is the Something More that I am seeking? What is my ultimate good? Let me recommit myself to it.

> When Jesus turned and saw them following, he said to them, "What are you looking for?"
>
> *John 1:38*

READINGS:
1 John 3:7–10; John 1:35–42

THURSDAY, January 5
JOHN NEUMANN, BISHOP

Transparency

In today's gospel Jesus calls Nathanael a man "without deceit"; some translations use the phrase "without guile." In other words, Nathanael is one of those transparent persons that one encounters and knows immediately. In the language of the Johari Window, he is one of those completely open persons: known by himself and known by others.

Transparent people are the most free—the most giving of themselves and the most accepting of others. We desire to be that way but often fall short, having some "guile" mixed into our personalities. Yet we seek to enlarge the transparent quality of ourselves.

If transparency is a value, how can I make it grow in my own actions and relationships? Let me ask God to give me an open heart.

> Let us love, not in word or speech, but in truth and action....For God is greater than our hearts, and he knows everything.
>
> *1 John 3:18, 20*

READINGS:
1 John 3:11–21; John 1:43–51

FRIDAY, January 6
ANDRÉ BESSETTE, RELIGIOUS

Welcome to the christological debates of the first century. Scholars believe today's first reading was written in opposition to "spiritualist" Christians who felt that simply "having the Spirit" was enough for salvation. On the contrary, says the author of 1 John, we need to get involved in the world. We need flesh and blood: moral choices, death and dying. We need Jesus, because he "is the one who came by water and blood...not with the water only but with the water and the blood" (1 John 5:6).

Carnality and our connection with the human race is the true realm of salvation. Jesus showed us the way. Simply being "enlightened" is insufficient. Loving others is the answer.

Do I sometimes take undue satisfaction in just being a Catholic, or Christian, or whatever? What steps can I take to shake off this self-congratulatory attitude? Let me recommit myself to a walk with suffering humanity.

> Whoever has the Son has life; whoever does not have the Son of God does not have life.
>
> *1 John 5:12*

READINGS:
1 John 5:5–13; Mark 1:7–11

SATURDAY, January 7
RAYMOND OF PEÑAFORT, PRIEST

Jesus, the wine

Weddings are wonderful—especially the wedding of the transcendent God with the human race. That is the larger event that underlies today's gospel story. Human life is good, but something is lacking in it. Mary notices. She doesn't precisely ask Jesus; she merely points out, "They have no wine" (John 2:2). So Jesus provides the wine: wonderful wine, far surpassing human expectations.

So it is with the incarnation. God pours out wine for us in the form of his Son. God joins the human celebration and raises it to a higher and more exalted level than we could conceive of by ourselves. God's imagination surpasses our own.

Now, as we approach the end of the Christmas season, it is appropriate to stop and give thanks for what we have been given.

Think of the happiest moment in your life. Now think of God infusing it with God's own life, joining our celebration, laughing and singing with us. In prayer, express your gratitude.

READINGS:
1 John 5:14–21; John 2:1–11

SUNDAY, January 8
EPIPHANY

We are probably like the Magi. We know when something big is in the works, but usually the questions we ask about it are too small. The Magi came asking the question, "Where is the child who has been born king of the Jews?" (Matt 2:2). They found more than just a king—and far more than the king of the Jews. This child was born for all peoples and nations.

We come to God with our needs and worries. God's answer is always much larger than our questions. Don't worry about daily life, God seems to tell us. The life I can give you is greater and deeper than that. I will lift up your life and make it part of mine.

There are no membership requirements, no initiation fees. No one pays attention to the way you look or speak. You don't need a green card. Come just the way you are.

Is my notion of God's kingdom too limited? How can I help break down the walls people build around it?

> Gentiles have become fellow heirs, members of the same body, and sharers in the promise.
>
> *Ephesians 3:6*

READINGS:
Isa 60:1–6; Eph 3:2–3a, 5–6; Matt 2:1–12

MONDAY, January 9
THE BAPTISM OF THE LORD

A light to the nations

Take down the Christmas tree. Put away the lights. Wrap up each of the figures from the crèche—the Magi and the camels. Take down the Christmas cards and put them in a box, then put the box under the bed. The Christmas season is over.

Jesus must have felt something like this after he was baptized in the Jordan. The long period of preparation in Nazareth had come to an end. Henceforth, he would be thrust into the daily business of preaching the kingdom, healing the broken, and—oh, yes—suffering and dying. The salad days were over.

God's message to us is pretty much as it was to him then. Ordinary time is looming—and beyond it, somewhere, Lent and then Good Friday. There is a lot of work to be done and not much time to do it. Our mandate has been given to us by Isaiah:

> I have given you as a covenant to the people,
> a light to the nations,
> to open the eyes that are blind,
> to bring out the prisoners from the dungeon,
> from the prison those who sit in darkness.
>
> *Isaiah 42:6–7*

It's time to get to work!

READINGS:
Isa 42:1–4, 6–7; Mark 1:7–11